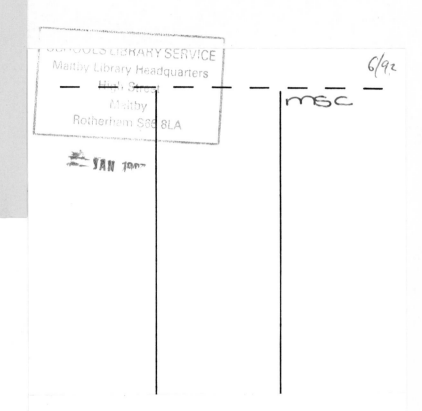

ROTHERHAM PUBLIC LIBRARIES

This book must be returned by the date specified at the time of issue as the Date Due for Return.
The loan may be extended (personally, by post or telephone) for a further period, if the book is not required by another reader, by quoting the above number   LM1 (C)

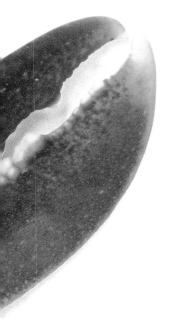

Amazing Armoured Animals

WRITTEN BY
SANDIE SOWLER

PHOTOGRAPHED BY
JERRY YOUNG
& JANE BURTON

DORLING KINDERSLEY
London · New York · Stuttgart

A Dorling Kindersley Book

Project editor Louise Pritchard
Art editor Toni Rann
Senior art editor Julia Harris
Senior editor Helen Parker
Production Shelagh Gibson

Illustrations by Dan Wright and Jane Gedye
Animals supplied by Trevor Smith's Animal World;
Steve Derham (pp 14-15); Dorking Aquatics (pp 8-9, 18-19, 26-27)
Editorial consultant Joyce Pope
Special thanks to Bristol Zoo, Cotswold Wildlife Park and Edward Wade
Carl Gombrich for research

First published in Great Britain in 1992 by
Dorling Kindersley Limited
9 Henrietta Street, London WC2E 8PS

A CIP catalogue record for this book
is available from the British Library

ISBN 0-86318-733 1

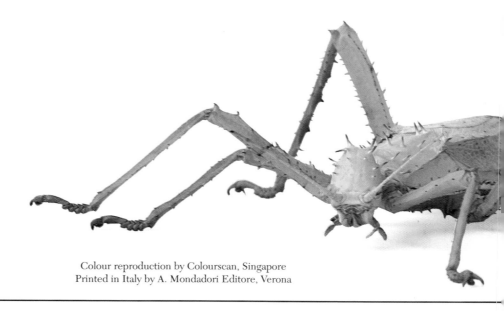

Colour reproduction by Colourscan, Singapore
Printed in Italy by A. Mondadori Editore, Verona

Contents

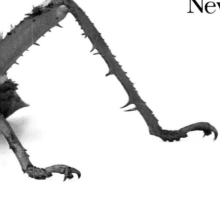

 # Why have armour?

Most animals have skin to protect their body, and skin can be tough. Many animals have extra protection, or armour. But this armour does not always work – sometimes hungry enemies find ways to break through the armour.

Lobster march
Armour can be more effective if animals join forces. Every year spiny lobsters march together in single file across the open seabed to deeper water.

The shell of this edible crab is about 20 cm wide

Armour covers the whole of this crab including its legs

All boxed up
Life underwater is no safer than life on land so there are armoured animals in the water too. Sea turtles have a thick shell which protects their whole body except the head and flippers.

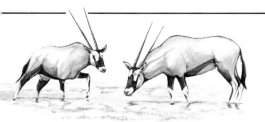

elf-defence
ome animals will try to fight off an
nemy if they are cornered and
annot run any further. A weapon of
ome sort can then come in handy.
emsboks have been known to stab
ons with their dagger-like horns.

Light as a feather
Most birds and bats
do not have any
armour as it would
make them too
heavy to fly. Even
a bird's beak is as
light as possible.

*Claw for catching food
and for self-defence*

Hard hat
Many animals need armour
because of the way they live.
The cassowary of Australia
pushes through thick bushes
head first, so it has a bony
helmet to protect its head.
It can run at up to 45 km/h
– but it cannot fly.

keleton protection
unting animals,
lled predators,
d it harder
get a meal if the
eal is protected in a hard
at. This crab has a tough
tside skeleton which helps
protect it against creatures
oking for a quick snack.

Thick skinned
Being large
like a hippopotamus can help to put off a
hungry predator. But if a crocodile should
dare to attack a hippo, the hippo's thick skin
protects it against the crocodile's teeth.

Protective clothing

Some animals have extra-thick skin. This protects them against enemies, against stings and bites, against the weather, or sometimes just against wear and tear.

This male white rhinoceros is about 1.7 m tall

Thick folds

The Indian rhinoceros looks as if it is wearing a suit of armour. But it really just has very thick skin which hangs in folds. There is even a special fold of skin to protect its tail!

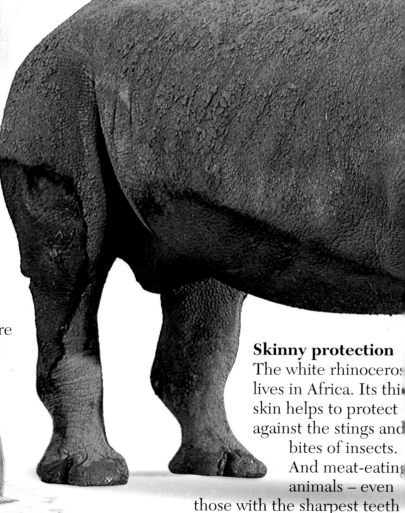

Fat and warm

Walruses live in the Arctic where it is very cold. They often sit on an ice block floating on the sea. To keep them warm, walruses have lots of fat called blubber and a thick skin.

Skinny protection

The white rhinoceros lives in Africa. Its thick skin helps to protect against the stings and bites of insects. And meat-eating animals – even those with the sharpest teeth rarely bother to attack it.

nose for food

aardvark's thick skin protects it against the stings
angry ants and termites which it eats. With ears
a rabbit's and a nose like a pig's, the aardvark uses
strong sense of smell and hearing to find its food.

*Horns to help put off
an enemy. They are
made of glued-
together hair*

On your knees

Warthogs have a patch of
thick skin on the front of their
legs as they often get down on their "knees"
to eat. This way they can reach grass in
awkward places, such as under a thorny bush.

Hurt me if you can

A honey badger eats anything it
can lay its teeth on, from young
antelopes to honey. It is well
protected by its skin. No sting,
tooth, claw, or quill can pierce it.

11

Prickles

Spines may look awkward to carry around all the time, but they protect the wearer from becoming someone's supper. Only a few animals have found a way of getting round the prickles and eating the meal inside.

Don't touch me!
If a shadow falls on a hat-pin sea urchin, the urchin's long spines turn towards the shadow to put off a possible attacker. The spines can break off in an enemy's flesh, causing great pain.

Nostrils at the end of the beak sniff out food

This spiny anteater is about 60 cm long including its tail

Prickly clean
A hedgehog has up to 7,000 spines. These are such good protection that the hedgehog has few natural enemies. What's more, the spines do not get tangled, or dirty.

Tricky meal

The North American fisher is a weasel-like mammal. It knows how to get a tasty meal out of a bundle of spines. It flips the porcupine over to get at its spineless tummy.

Baby rattle

Tenrecs are small mammals which live in Madagascar. Some kinds are spiny. A young common tenrec relies on its barbed spines to protect it against predators. It can also rub its spines together to make a noise, letting its mother know where it is.

Spiky customer

Even some fish are prickly. The lionfish has spines along its back and in its fins. A predator that gets too close may get spiked by the spines. It will never forget the poisonous sting the fish gives it.

Spiny and egg-laying

When the spiny anteater is in danger, it quickly digs down into the ground until only the tip of its extremely sharp spines are showing. The spiny anteater is an unusual mammal – the female lays eggs.

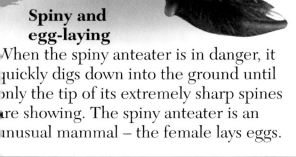

Some hair!

The spines of mammals are specially adapted hairs. They grow out of the skin just as fur does. This tree porcupine from South America has a partly spineless tail so it can use it to cling on to branches.

Scales

*Spiny-tailed lizards li
in the desert, where
it is more than 40° C
in the shade*

Some animals have an armour of protective scales. Some kinds of scales overlap, some are joined edge to edge. Some are extra thick, others are pointed or ridged. Many give their wearer a brightly coloured coat.

Tail weapon
Guess why this lizard is called a spiny-tailed lizard! If it is attacked, it may try to fight off its enemy by lashing its spiky tail. The spikes are really large, pointed scales.

Doubly useful
Snakes, such as this pine snake, have scaly skin. As well as giving protection, the scales help the snake to grip the ground as it wriggles along.

Toughened scales
Crocodiles and alligators, like this black caiman, have heavy scales. The caiman's back has an extra armour of thick bony plates.

Waterproof
This photo shows the spiny-tailed lizard's scales. They protect t lizard's waterproof ski

nells awful

he pangolin is a mammal,
ut it looks more like a
-cone. Its whole body is
overed in overlapping,
ale-like plates. If an
nemy isn't discouraged
y this armour, the
angolin can squirt a
usty-smelling liquid.

Scaly legs

All birds have scales on
their legs. The ostrich
has very thick scales on
the front of its legs. The
ostrich cannot fly, and
the scales protect its
legs as it runs through
the small, thorny
bushes where it lives.

Your scales or your life

Some scales protect their owner by
coming off. A silverfish is an insect
that is covered with waxy scales.
Sometimes it escapes
being eaten by shedding
some of this armour –
leaving its enemy with
a mouthful of scales.

*From nose to tail,
this spiny-tailed
lizard is about
23 cm long*

*ong toes
nd claws
r digging
urrows in
he sand*

Fish in a box

Fish have scales which are not
part of the skin but are attached
to the skin. Boxfish are enclosed
in a stiff case of bony plates like
a box. Living inside a box makes
it hard to move so boxfish are
not very speedy swimmers!

Hidden protection

Many animals look easy prey. But some have a surprise in store for any hungry hunters looking for their dinner.

Cut and thrust

The surgeon fish looks harmless, but hidden in a groove on either side of its tail is a razor-sharp spine. If the fish is disturbed, it lashes its tail. The spines stick out and cut any predator foolish enough to attack.

Groove containing spine

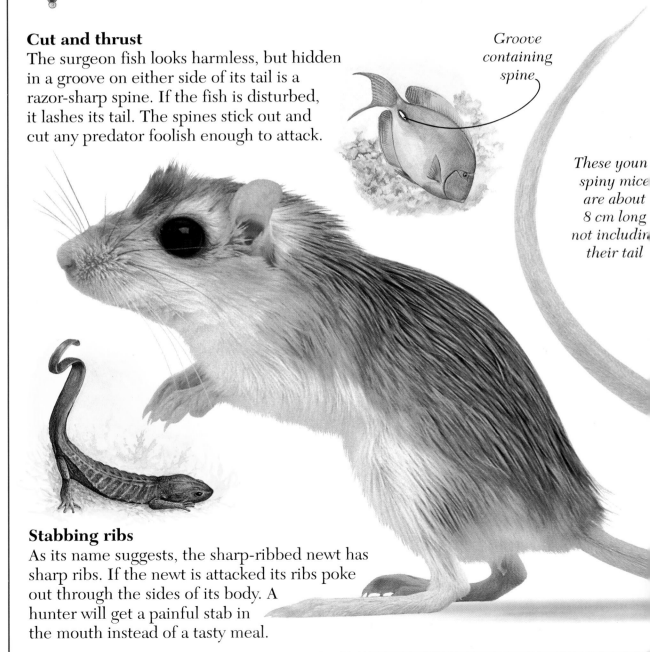

These youn[g] spiny mice are about 8 cm long not includi[ng] their tail[s]

Stabbing ribs

As its name suggests, the sharp-ribbed newt has sharp ribs. If the newt is attacked its ribs poke out through the sides of its body. A hunter will get a painful stab in the mouth instead of a tasty meal.

Sticks its neck out

Hidden under the skin on a potto's neck is a set of lumpy bones. If in danger, the potto tries to hide by keeping very still. But if attacked, it arches its neck to raise the hard bones in defence.

Standing firm

The hero shrew of Africa has a kind of internal armour – an amazingly strong backbone. It is said that a grown man can stand on the shrew without squashing it.

...nkles with spurs

...male platypus has a sharp claw-...e spine on the back of each ...nkle". These spines are usually ...cked away under a fold of skin, ...t if the platypus is attacked, it ...cks out, raising its spines to ...ject its enemy with poison.

...npleasant surprise

...spiny mouse's coat is not as ...ft as it looks. Its fur is stiff ...d spiky which ...akes it very ...pleasant ...eat!

Second-hand stings

This sea slug looks soft and easy to bite. But it has a clever defence. The stinging cells of the sea slug's favourite meal of jellyfish pass into its skin and work for it as efficiently as they did for their old owner.

Snails and seashells

One of the best kinds of armour in the animal world belongs to snails and other molluscs. Most of them have a hard outer covering called a shell. The shell has one or two parts and protects a soft body inside.

Mighty mollusc

The giant clam is the largest mollusc in the world. The two parts of its shell can grow to over 1.4 m wide. But clams take a long time to reach this size and some are hundreds of years old.

Giant land snail

Garden snail

Land giant

The shell of the giant African land snail grows to over 10 cm long – huge compared to a garden snail.

Tight fit

A limpet always goes back to the same place on a rock. It fits itself into a shallow pit made in the rock by the edge of its shell. And it clings so tightly it is almost impossible to remove.

Sitting tenant

Hermit crabs find that mollusc shells give excellent second-hand protection. Unlike most crabs the hermit crab does not have its own shell. So it sets up home inside empty seashells.

A hinge joins the two halves of the shell together

Hinged protection

If in danger, a scallop can clap its shells together hard, forcing water out. This action shoots the scallop forwards, away from the danger. But if there's no time to escape, the scallop keeps its shell shut tight.

The scallop's tentacles are very sensitive to touch

Weight problem

Snails that live in water have a thicker, heavier shell than land snails but the water supports some of the weight. Land snails have to carry all the weight of their shell themselves.

Smash and grab

Song thrushes have a clever way of getting at the tasty body of a snail. They hold the snail in their beak and smash the shell against a stone.

Killer shell

A wise animal will not touch a cone shell. Not only is this mollusc protected by its shell, but it is deadly poisonous. It has a dart-like tooth inside its shell which it brings out to attack passing fish for its food.

This flame scallop is about 8 cm wide

Insects

All insects have a strong skin called an exoskeleton which supports and protects them. The exoskeleton is necessary as insects live in a dangerous world. Birds, mammals, reptiles, amphibians, spiders, and even other insects all eat insect for dinner.

Protecting the young

Insects change from egg to larva to pupa to adult. Many kinds of caterpillar, such as this American moth caterpillar, have stinging spines to protect them.

Small wings show that this jungle nymph is a female

It's a stick-up

One kick from a weta can cause a nasty wound. These rare insects from New Zealand have strong spiny legs which they raise up in the air to frighten a predator. And woe betide the predator that is too close.

This jungle nymph is about 16 cm long with 10-cm-long legs

Wax works

Some scale insects cover themselves with a special wax which acts as an extra suit of armour. Scale insects also make a sugary substance that ants seem to like to eat.

Mouthful of spikes

This jungle nymph's hard exoskeleton makes a good suit of armour. This insect's body and legs are fringed with sharp, hooked spikes. A predator that tries to take a bite will get a painful mouthful.

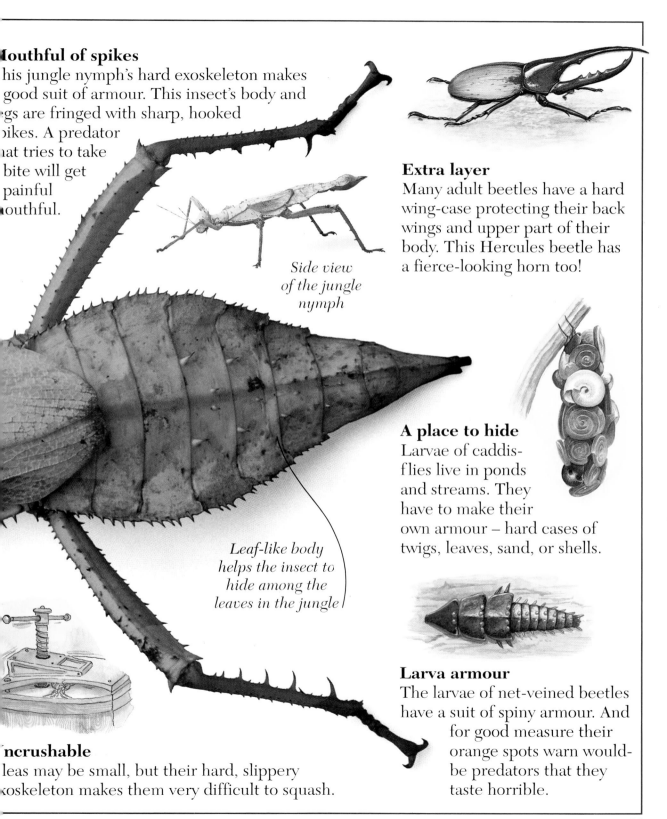

Side view of the jungle nymph

Leaf-like body helps the insect to hide among the leaves in the jungle

Extra layer

Many adult beetles have a hard wing-case protecting their back wings and upper part of their body. This Hercules beetle has a fierce-looking horn too!

A place to hide

Larvae of caddis-flies live in ponds and streams. They have to make their own armour – hard cases of twigs, leaves, sand, or shells.

Larva armour

The larvae of net-veined beetles have a suit of spiny armour. And for good measure their orange spots warn would-be predators that they taste horrible.

Uncrushable

Fleas may be small, but their hard, slippery exoskeleton makes them very difficult to squash.

Armadillos

When Spanish soldiers invaded South America in the 16th century they saw some strange animals which they could easily have mistaken for small dinosaurs. They called them armadillos, meaning little armoured ones.

Armour plated

Armadillos have a suit of bony plates growing in the skin. This helps to protect them against their enemies. This hairy armadillo has a thin covering of hair as well as its armour. The hair grows between the plates.

This hairy armadillo is about 45 cm long, not including its tail

Fairies and giants

There are 20 different kinds of armadillo. They include the fairy armadillo which could fit in your hands, and the giant armadillo which is as big as a small pig.

Doorstop

A fairy armadillo has a flat circular piece of armour on its bottom. When it is scared the armadillo burrows quickly into the ground until only its bottom is showing. The circle of armour blocks the entrance to the burrow, protecting the armadillo inside.

Powerful front legs and claws feet are used for digging

Foursome

Armadillos have between one and 12 young a year. The babies are born with a soft, leathery skin which hardens in a few weeks. The nine-banded armadillo usually has a set of four identical babies every year.

Sink or swim

An armadillo can cross a small river in two ways. It can walk underwater along the river-bed, or it can swim. It makes itself float by gulping air into its tummy.

Speedy digger

Armadillos use their excellent sense of smell to find ants, termites, or other insects to eat. They dig as fast as they can to catch the ants, jamming their nose into the soil at the same time. They don't bother to breathe – they can hold their breath for up to six minutes.

Hiding away

A pill woodlouse rolling up into a ball

Many kinds of animals do not need to find a place to hide when they are in danger. They can curl up into a tight ball or coil, or hide in their own shell, protecting the soft parts of their body.

Walking prickles
If danger threatens, the first thing a hedgehog will do is stick up its spines and wait for the danger to pass. If this doesn't work, it can curl up into a tight spiny ball.

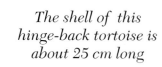

Hinge to allow shell to bend

A perfect fit
If in danger, the three-banded armadillo rolls itself up. Its head, tail, and body armour fit so well together that no gap is left through which an enemy can break in.

Strong legs needed to support the heavy shell

The shell of this hinge-back tortoise is about 25 cm long

Hinge-back tortoise hiding away

trong box

ortoises can pull their head,
gs, and tail into their shell
hen they want to hide. This
nge-back tortoise can go one
ep further. It can bend the
ack of its shell downwards
ving it even more protection.

Safe inside

Snails hide in
their shell too.
Some snails
have a piece of
shell called an operculum
(*oh-per-cue-lum*). They go into their shell
and use their operculum to shut the door.

Operculum

Ocean rollers

With its linked pieces of shell, the
chiton looks as if it is wearing a suit
of mail, or armour. It is often called
the coat-of-mail shell. If it is knocked
off its rock it quickly curls up and
can be rolled around by the sea
without being harmed.

On Mum's tail

A mother pangolin
often carries her
baby on her tail. If
danger threatens,
she curls round the
baby protecting it
and herself in a ball
of hard, bony scales.

Hard pill to swallow

If attacked, the pill millipede
curls into a ball. Its enemies,
such as ants and beetles, cannot get a grip on this
smooth "pill" so they look for something else to eat.

New coats of armour

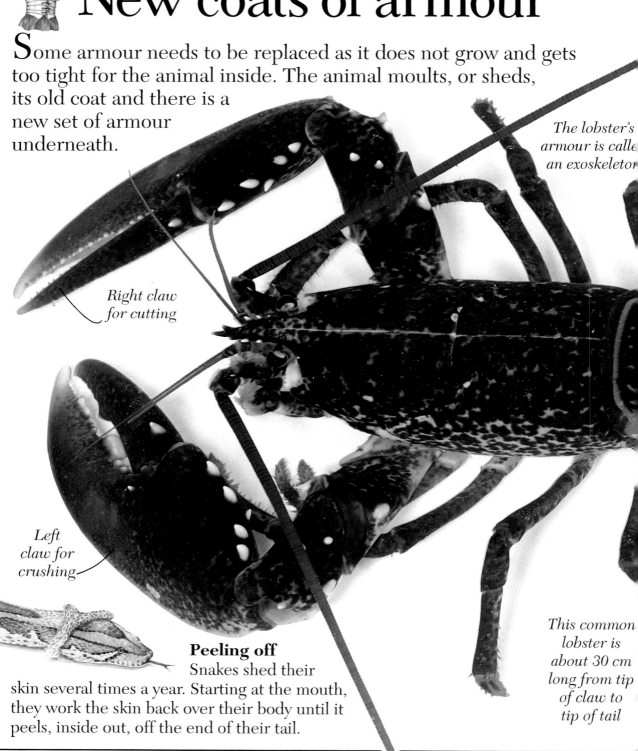

Some armour needs to be replaced as it does not grow and gets too tight for the animal inside. The animal moults, or sheds, its old coat and there is a new set of armour underneath.

The lobster's armour is called an exoskeleton

Right claw for cutting

Left claw for crushing

Peeling off
Snakes shed their skin several times a year. Starting at the mouth, they work the skin back over their body until it peels, inside out, off the end of their tail.

This common lobster is about 30 cm long from tip of claw to tip of tail

From water to air

A young dragonfly, or nymph, lives in water and cannot fly. As it grows, it sheds its exoskeleton several times. Finally, the insect crawls out – as a beautiful adult dragonfly with wings.

Red deer stag

1 year old   *3 years old*

Falling velvet

5 years old

Part-time headgear

Every autumn, the velvet covering on the antlers of a stag, or male red deer, dries up and falls off. In winter, the whole set of antlers falls off. A new – usually bigger – set grows the next year.

Tight jacket

When it gets too tight, a lobster's shell splits across the back, and the lobster pulls itself out – legs and all. It must stay out of danger for a few days while its new armour hardens.

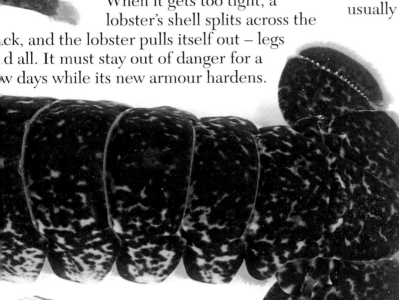

Growing claw

If a crab or lobster loses a claw or a leg it can start to grow a new one the next time it sheds its shell. But it takes several moults for the new claw to grow to its full size.

Outside   *Inside*

Living rooms

The shell of a snail is always growing so the animal does not need to shed it. But a nautilus lives in one chamber of its shell. As the shell grows, the animal seals off the old chamber and moves into a new one.

Patchy skin

Lizards shed their scaly skin in bits and pieces. They look a bit messy with skin hanging off! But their smart new skin will make up for it.

Weapons

Many animals have their own personal weapons which they use to defend their home, their young, and themselves. But some fierce-looking weapons are only used by males to win females, or just for showing off!

Keep away!
A sting is a useful weapon if you want to stop someone squashing you! A wasp uses its sting for this purpose and to attack any animal that threatens its nes[t]

This ram is a Jacob's sheep. It is just over 1 m tall. Unlike most horned animals, it has four horns rather than two

Battering ram
A sheep's horns are made of bone covered in a hard, horny sleeve. The male sheep, or ram, uses its big horns for fighting other rams. The ram charge at each othe clashing horn and heads.

rength in numbers

usk oxen have sharp up-
rving horns. If they are
tacked by wolves they
rm a circle with their
ung in the middle and get
ady to defend themselves.

Face guard

The babirusa pig defends
itself with four long, sharp
tusks. Two grow out
of the top of its snout
making a cage in front
of its face. A legend says
that, at night, the pig hangs
by its tusks from a tree!

*This horn is about
30 cm long*

Ancient tail

Some reptiles, such as
crocodiles, use their tail in
self-defence. But no living
reptile has a tail like that of
some of the dinosaurs.
Stegosaurus had spikes
of 50 cm long on its tail.

eavy protection

ephant tusks are the heaviest teeth in
e world. Each one can weigh as
uch as an adult human being.
ephants use their tusks to get
od and to defend
eir young against
y animal bold
ough to attack.

Index